iPhone 14 Pro User Guide Made Easy for Beginners

Essential and Advanced Features of iPhone 14 Pro

By

Andrew Sylvan
Copyright@2023

Table of Contents

CHAPTER 1

Setting Up Your iPhone 14 Pro

Setting up your iPhone 14 Pro is an exciting and important process that ensures you can make the most out of your new device.

1. Powering On:

   - Locate the power button on the side of your iPhone 14 Pro.

   - Press and hold the power button until the Apple logo appears on the screen.

- Release the power button and wait for the device to boot up.

2. Language Selection:

    - On the Welcome screen, you will be prompted to choose your preferred language.

    - Swipe up or down to scroll through the list of available languages.

    - Tap on your desired language to select it.

3. Wi-Fi Network Connection:

    - If you have a Wi-Fi network available, you

will be prompted to
connect to it.

- Tap on your desired
  Wi-Fi network from the
  list.

- Enter the Wi-Fi
  password if required.

- Tap "Join" to connect
  to the network.

4. Data Transfer Options:

- If you are upgrading
  from a previous iPhone
  or Android device, you
  can choose to transfer
  your data to the new
  iPhone 14 Pro.

- Select your preferred
  method of data transfer:

a. Quick Start: If you have your old iPhone nearby, you can use Quick Start to transfer data wirelessly.

b. Move Data from Android: If you are switching from an Android device, you can use the "Move Data from Android" option.

c. Restore from iCloud Backup: If you have an iCloud backup of your previous device, you can choose to restore from it.

d. Set Up as New iPhone: If you want to start with a clean slate,

you can set up your
iPhone as a new device.

5. Face ID or Touch ID Setup:

- The iPhone 14 Pro
  offers biometric
  authentication options
  for added security and
  convenience.

- Follow the on-screen
  instructions to set up
  Face ID or Touch ID
  based on your
  preference.

- For Face ID: Position
  your face within the
  frame and move your
  head in a circular
  motion to complete the
  scan.

- For Touch ID: Follow the instructions to place and lift your finger on the designated area to capture your fingerprint.

6. Apple ID Sign-in or Create New Apple ID:

- Sign in with your existing Apple ID by entering your Apple ID email address and password.

- If you don't have an Apple ID, tap "Don't have an Apple ID or forgot it?" and follow the prompts to create a new Apple ID.

- Alternatively, you can choose to set up the iPhone without an Apple ID by tapping "Set Up Later in Settings."

7. Terms and Conditions:

- Read and review the Terms and Conditions presented on the screen.

- Tap "Agree" to proceed if you agree to the terms.

- You may be prompted to enter your Apple ID password or passcode to confirm your agreement.

8. Siri Setup:

  - Decide whether you want to enable Siri, Apple's virtual assistant.

  - Tap "Continue" to set up Siri or tap "Turn On Siri Later" if you prefer to set it up later.

  - Follow the on-screen prompts to set up Siri preferences, including your voice activation method.

9. Screen Time:

  - Screen Time provides insights into your device usage and allows you to set limits for app and device usage.

- Tap "Continue" to set up Screen Time or tap "Set Up Later in Settings" to skip this step.

- Follow the on-screen prompts to set up Screen Time preferences, including app limits, downtime, and content restrictions.

10.   Apple Pay Setup:

- If you want to use Apple Pay for contactless payments, you can set it up during

the initial setup
process.

- Tap "Continue" to set
  up Apple Pay or tap
  "Set Up Later in
  Wallet" to skip this
  step.

- Follow the on-screen
  instructions to add your
  credit or debit cards to
  Apple Pay.

11.   App Analytics and
True Tone Display:

- Decide whether you
  want to share app
  analytics with Apple
  and whether you want
  to enable True Tone
  display technology.

- Tap "Continue" to proceed or tap "Customize Settings" to adjust your preferences.

12. Display Zoom and Text Size:

- Choose your preferred display zoom level and text size for optimal readability.

- Tap on the different options to preview and select the one that suits your preferences.

13. Dark Mode:

- Decide whether you want to enable Dark Mode, which provides a dark color scheme for the device interface.

- Tap "Continue" to enable Dark Mode or tap "Light Appearance" to keep the default light mode.

14. iCloud Keychain:

- Choose whether to enable iCloud Keychain, which securely stores and syncs your passwords and payment information across devices.

- Tap "Continue" to set up iCloud Keychain or tap "Set Up Later in

Settings" to skip this step.

15.   Find My:

- Decide whether you want to enable the Find My feature, which helps you locate your device if it's lost or stolen.

- Tap "Continue" to set up Find My or tap "Set Up Later in Settings" to skip this step.

16.   Display Zoom and Text Size:

- Choose your preferred display zoom level and text size for optimal readability.

- Tap on the different options to preview and select the one that suits your preferences.

17.   Dark Mode:

- Decide whether you want to enable Dark Mode, which provides a dark color scheme for the device interface.

- Tap "Continue" to enable Dark Mode or tap "Light Appearance" to keep the default light mode.

18.   iCloud Keychain:

- Choose whether to enable iCloud Keychain, which

securely stores and syncs your passwords and payment information across devices.

- Tap "Continue" to set up iCloud Keychain or tap "Set Up Later in Settings" to skip this step.

19. Find My:

- Decide whether you want to enable the Find My feature, which helps you locate your device if it's lost or stolen.

- Tap "Continue" to set up Find My or tap "Set

Up Later in Settings" to
skip this step.

20.   Apple News and App
Suggestions:

- Decide whether you
  want to enable Apple
  News and receive
  personalized app
  suggestions.

- Tap "Continue" to
  enable these features or
  tap "Not Now" to skip
  this step.

21.   Screen Time for Family
Members:

- If you want to set up
  Screen Time for family
  members, you can do
  so by tapping "Set Up

Screen Time for
Family" and following
the prompts.

22.   Data & Privacy:

- Review and select your
  preferred data and
  privacy settings.

- Tap "Continue" to
  proceed or tap
  "Customize Settings" to
  adjust specific
  preferences.

23.   App Analytics and
Share with App Developers:

- Decide whether you
  want to share app
  analytics with Apple
  and whether you want

to allow app developers to contact you.

- Tap "Continue" to proceed or tap "Customize Settings" to adjust your preferences.

24.   Apple Music:

- If you have an Apple Music subscription or want to sign up for one, you can choose to set it up now or skip this step by tapping "Set Up Later in Music."

25.   Apple TV+ and Apple Arcade:

- Decide whether you want to start a free trial

or subscribe to Apple TV+ or Apple Arcade.

- Tap "Continue" to set up these services or tap "Set Up Later in Settings" to skip this step.

26.   Siri Suggestions:

- Choose whether you want Siri to provide personalized suggestions based on your usage.

- Tap "Continue" to enable Siri Suggestions or tap "Not Now" to skip this step.

27.   App Tracking Transparency:

- Decide whether you want to allow apps to request permission to track your activity across other companies' apps and websites.

- Tap "Continue" to enable App Tracking Transparency or tap "Ask App Not to Track" to limit tracking.

28.   Screen Time Passcode:

- Set a passcode for Screen Time if you want to prevent unauthorized access to Screen Time settings.

- Follow the on-screen instructions to create a passcode and confirm it.

29.   iCloud Drive:

- Choose whether you want to enable iCloud Drive, which allows you to store files in the cloud and access them across devices.

- Tap "Continue" to set up iCloud Drive or tap "Not Now" to skip this step.

30.   Siri Voice:

- Select your preferred Siri voice from the available options.

- Tap on the voice to preview and choose the one you prefer.

31. Appearance:

- Choose between light or dark appearance for the device interface.

- Tap on your preferred appearance to select it.

32. Accessibility:

- If you require accessibility features, tap "Continue" to set them up or tap "Set Up Later in Accessibility" to skip this step.

33. Zoom Display:

- Enable or disable the zoom display feature, which magnifies the screen content for better visibility.

- Tap "Continue" to set up zoom display or tap "Not Now" to skip this step.

34.   Apple Pay Cash:

- Decide whether you want to set up Apple Pay Cash, which allows you to send and receive money using Apple Pay.

- Tap "Continue" to set up Apple Pay Cash or tap "Set Up Later in

Wallet" to skip this step.

35.   Home Screen Layout:

- Choose between the standard app layout or the new App Library view for organizing your apps.

- Tap on your preferred option to select it.

36.   Finalize Setup:

- Review the summary of your chosen settings and configurations.

- Tap "Get Started" to complete the setup process and access the home screen of your iPhone 14 Pro.

CHAPTER 2

Essential Features of iPhone 14 Pro

Home Screen Navigation:

The home screen of the iPhone 14 Pro serves as the central hub for accessing your apps, widgets, and other features. It provides a simple and intuitive interface that allows you to navigate through your device efficiently. Here are some essential features of home screen navigation:

1. App Icons: The home screen displays various app icons representing the applications installed on your iPhone 14

Pro. You can tap on an app icon to launch the corresponding app. The app icons can be rearranged, organized into folders, or placed on additional home screen pages for easy access.

2. App Library: Introduced in iOS 14, the App Library is a feature that automatically organizes your apps into categories, making it easier to find and access them. By swiping right on the home screen or by using the search bar at the top, you can access the App Library and browse through your apps in a more organized manner.

3. Search Bar: Located at the top of the home screen, the search bar allows you to quickly search for apps, contacts, messages, emails, and more. Simply tap on the search bar and enter your search query to find what you're looking for.

4. Today View: By swiping right on the home screen or by pulling down from the top of the screen, you can access the Today View. This section provides widgets that display relevant information such as weather updates, calendar events, news headlines, and more. You can customize the widgets and their placement

in the Today View according to your preferences.

5. Notification Center: By swiping down from the top edge of the screen, you can access the Notification Center. This area displays your recent notifications, including missed calls, messages, app alerts, and other important updates. You can tap on a notification to open the corresponding app or use 3D Touch (if available) to access quick actions or preview content.

Control Center:

The Control Center is a convenient feature on the iPhone 14 Pro that provides quick access to various settings and controls without having to navigate through multiple menus. It offers a range of essential features and shortcuts that enhance your device's functionality. Here are some key aspects of the Control Center:

1. Accessing the Control Center: To access the Control Center, simply swipe down from the top-right corner of the screen. Alternatively, on devices with a Home button, you can swipe up from the bottom of the screen. This action reveals the Control Center panel, which is displayed as a card-like overlay.

2. Control Center Modules: The Control Center is divided into modules, each representing a different control or setting. Some common modules include:

- Wi-Fi and Bluetooth: Control and manage wireless connectivity.

- Brightness: Adjust the screen brightness.

- Volume: Control the media and ringer volume.

- Do Not Disturb: Activate or deactivate the Do Not Disturb mode.

- Airdrop: Share files
  and media with nearby
  devices.

- Screen Mirroring:
  Mirror your iPhone's
  screen to an external
  display or Apple TV.

- Flashlight: Turn on the
  built-in LED flash as a
  flashlight.

- Camera: Quickly
  launch the camera app
  for capturing photos or
  videos.

- Timer: Set a timer for
  specific durations.

- Calculator: Access a
  basic calculator for
  quick calculations.

- Airplay: Stream audio or video to compatible devices.

3. Customization: You can customize the Control Center to include or remove specific modules according to your preferences. This allows you to tailor the Control Center to include the controls and shortcuts you use most frequently. To customize the Control Center, go to Settings > Control Center > Customize Controls.

4. Expanded Controls: Some modules in the Control Center provide additional options or settings when expanded. For example,

expanding the Music module reveals playback controls, album artwork, and access to playlists. Similarly, expanding the Connectivity module provides quick access to additional Wi-Fi networks or Bluetooth devices for easy switching.

5. Home Controls: If you have smart home devices compatible with Apple's HomeKit framework, the Control Center can serve as a central hub for controlling and managing them. You can add home control modules to the Control Center, allowing you to control lights, thermostats, door locks, and

other supported devices with a simple tap.

6. Media Controls: When playing audio or video content from apps like Apple Music, Spotify, or YouTube, the Control Center displays media controls for easy playback management. You can play, pause, skip tracks, adjust volume, and even control playback on compatible devices using Airplay.

7. Accessibility Shortcut: The Control Center also provides a convenient way to access certain accessibility features. By customizing the Control Center, you can add

accessibility shortcuts for
functions like Voiceover,
Magnifier, Assistive Touch,
and more, making it easier
for users with specific
accessibility needs to quickly
enable or disable these
features.

8. Apple Wallet: The Control
Center includes a shortcut to
Apple Wallet, where you can
store and access your digital
passes, tickets, loyalty cards,
and payment information.
With a simple tap on the
Wallet module in the Control
Center, you can quickly
access your cards and make
contactless payments using
Apple Pay.

9. Quick Settings: The Control Center allows you to quickly toggle various settings on or off. This includes features like Airplane Mode, Cellular Data, Wi-Fi, Bluetooth, Orientation Lock, and more. By accessing the Control Center, you can conveniently enable or disable these settings without navigating through multiple menus.

10. Home Screen Orientation: Within the Control Center, you can find the Orientation Lock module, which allows you to lock the orientation of your device's screen. This prevents the screen from rotating when the device is tilted or turned,

ensuring a consistent viewing
experience.

Siri and Voice Control:

Siri and Voice Control are
powerful features of the iPhone 14
Pro that allow you to interact with
your device using voice commands.
They provide a convenient and
hands-free way to perform various
tasks, access information, and
control your device. Here are some
essential aspects of Siri and Voice
Control:

1. Siri Activation: To activate
    Siri, you can either press and
    hold the side button or say
    the "Hey Siri" phrase when
    your device is connected to
    power or when you have
    enabled the "Hey Siri"

feature. This triggers Siri and prompts it to listen for your command.

2. Voice Commands: With Siri, you can use natural language to ask questions, give instructions, and perform tasks. You can ask Siri to send messages, make phone calls, set reminders and alarms, schedule events, search the web, check the weather, play music, control smart home devices, and much more.

3. Personalized Assistance: Siri learns your preferences, habits, and context over time to provide personalized assistance. It can suggest

relevant actions, offer
proactive suggestions, and
provide tailored
recommendations based on
your usage patterns and
interactions.

4. Integration with Apps and
   Services: Siri integrates with
   a wide range of apps and
   services on your iPhone 14
   Pro. This enables you to
   perform specific tasks within
   supported apps using voice
   commands. For example, you
   can ask Siri to order food,
   book a ride, make a
   reservation, or send money
   using supported third-party
   apps.

5. Voice Feedback and Dictation: Siri provides voice feedback when responding to your queries or executing tasks. It can read out information, provide directions, and even engage in natural conversations. Additionally, Siri supports dictation, allowing you to dictate text messages, emails, notes, and more, making it easier to compose content using your voice.

6. Voice Control: Voice Control takes voice commands a step further by providing comprehensive control over your device using voice inputs. It enables users with mobility or accessibility

challenges to navigate the
device, launch apps, adjust
settings, and interact with on-
screen elements solely
through voice commands.

7. Accessibility Features: Siri
and Voice Control play a
crucial role in enhancing
accessibility on the iPhone 14
Pro. They enable users with
visual impairments, motor
disabilities, or other
accessibility needs to interact
with their device effectively
and independently.

Notifications and Do Not Disturb:

Notifications and Do Not Disturb
are essential features of the iPhone
14 Pro that help you manage

incoming alerts, stay informed, and control interruptions. They provide a balance between staying connected and maintaining focus when needed. Here are some key aspects of Notifications and Do Not Disturb:

1. Incoming Notifications: The iPhone 14 Pro displays notifications on the lock screen and in the Notification Center to keep you informed about new messages, emails, social media updates, calendar events, news, and more. Each app's notifications are grouped together for easy browsing.

2. Notification Management: You can customize how

notifications are displayed and organized. This includes options to prioritize notifications from specific apps or contacts, control whether notifications are shown on the lock screen, choose the notification style (banners, alerts, or badges), and manage notification grouping.

3. Notification Actions: Many notifications allow you to take actions directly from the notification itself, without opening the respective app. For example, you can reply to a message, archive an email, like a social media post, or snooze a reminder right from

the notification banner or
lock screen.

4. Notification Center: By
   swiping down from the top
   edge of the screen, you can
   access the Notification
   Center. This provides a
   chronological list of all your
   notifications, including those
   you might have missed. You
   can scroll through the
   notifications, clear them
   individually or in groups, and
   customize the information
   displayed in the Notification
   Center.

Do Not Disturb:

Do Not Disturb is a feature that allows you to temporarily silence notifications and prevent interruptions when you need uninterrupted focus or rest. Here are some key aspects of Do Not Disturb:

1. Manual Activation: You can manually activate Do Not Disturb mode by accessing the Control Center and tapping the crescent moon icon, or by going to Settings and enabling Do Not Disturb. When activated, notifications are silenced, and incoming calls are muted.

2. Scheduled Activation: Do Not Disturb can be scheduled

to automatically activate and deactivate at specific times. This is useful when you want to ensure uninterrupted sleep or concentration during certain hours. You can customize the schedule according to your preferences.

3. Bedtime Mode: In conjunction with the Clock app, Do Not Disturb offers a Bedtime Mode that silences notifications and dims the display during your scheduled sleep hours. It helps create a conducive environment for uninterrupted sleep and reduces disturbances caused by incoming alerts.

4. Allowances and Exceptions: Do Not Disturb allows you to customize its behavior by setting allowances and exceptions. You can choose to allow calls from specific contacts or repeated calls to ring through even when Do Not Disturb is active. This ensures important or urgent calls are not missed while still minimizing distractions.

5. Driving Mode: Do Not Disturb While Driving is a specialized mode that activates when your iPhone detects that you're driving. It automatically mutes notifications and sends an auto-reply to incoming messages, letting others know

that you're currently driving and will respond later.

6. Focus Modes: iOS 15 introduced Focus modes, which build upon the Do Not Disturb feature. Focus modes allow you to create customized profiles that determine which notifications and apps are allowed to interrupt you based on your chosen context. For example, you can have a Work mode that only allows work-related notifications, or a Personal mode that filters out work-related distractions.

7. Notification Summary: iOS 15 also introduced the Notification Summary

feature, which intelligently organizes and delivers non-urgent notifications in batches. This helps reduce interruptions by bundling less important notifications and delivering them at specific times of your choosing.

Multitasking:

Multitasking is a fundamental feature of the iPhone 14 Pro that allows you to efficiently switch between apps, work on multiple tasks simultaneously, and enhance productivity. Here are some essential aspects of multitasking on the iPhone 14 Pro:

1. App Switcher: The App Switcher is the primary tool for multitasking. To access it,

swipe up from the bottom of the screen and pause in the middle of the screen. This reveals the App Switcher, which displays a stack of recently used apps. You can swipe left or right to navigate through the app cards and tap on an app card to switch to it.

2. Split View: Split View allows you to have two apps open and active side by side on the screen. To activate Split View, open an app from the App Switcher, then swipe up from the bottom to access the Dock. Drag the second app from the Dock to the left or right edge of the screen until it snaps into place. This enables you to

simultaneously view and interact with both apps.

3. Slide Over: Slide Over is a feature that allows you to overlay a secondary app on top of the currently active app. To activate Slide Over, swipe up from the bottom of the screen to access the Dock, then drag the second app to the center of the screen. The secondary app appears in a floating window that can be moved around and interacted with while the primary app remains visible.

4. App Exposé: App Exposé provides an overview of all open windows or instances of a specific app. To access App

Exposé, swipe up from the bottom of the screen with multiple instances of an app open or perform a pinch-out gesture on the screen with multiple instances of an app. This displays all open instances of the app, allowing you to quickly switch between them or close specific instances.

5. Picture in Picture: Picture in Picture (PiP) allows you to continue watching videos or conducting FaceTime calls in a small floating window while using other apps. When a video is playing or a FaceTime call is active, you can swipe up from the bottom to minimize it into a smaller

window. This window can be moved around the screen, resized, and even hidden temporarily, allowing you to multitask without missing out on content.

6. App Previews: App Previews provide a quick way to access recently used apps without opening the App Switcher. To activate App Previews, swipe right from the left edge of the screen and release to switch to the previously used app. This allows for swift app switching and easy multitasking without navigating through the App Switcher.

7. Background App Refresh: iOS intelligently manages app background activity to balance performance and battery life. Background App Refresh allows apps to refresh their content in the background so that when you switch back to them, the latest information is already available. You can control which apps are allowed to refresh in the background by going to Settings > General > Background App Refresh.

8. Handoff: Handoff is a feature that enables seamless continuity between your iPhone, iPad, and Mac. It allows you to start a task on one device and continue it on

another. For example, you can begin writing an email on your iPhone and then pick up where you left off on your Mac. Handoff works with various apps, including Mail, Safari, Pages, Numbers, Keynote, and more.

9. Keyboard Shortcuts: The iPhone 14 Pro supports keyboard shortcuts, which can enhance multitasking and productivity. By connecting an external keyboard or using a compatible software keyboard, you can take advantage of keyboard shortcuts to perform actions like switching between apps, opening the App Switcher,

accessing the Control Center, and more.

10.   App Continuity: App Continuity is a feature that ensures a seamless experience when transitioning between different Apple devices. For example, if you're browsing a webpage on Safari on your iPhone, you can open Safari on your iPad or Mac and find the same webpage in the recently viewed tabs, allowing you to continue your browsing seamlessly.

These essential features of Siri and Voice Control, Notifications and Do Not Disturb, and Multitasking on the iPhone 14 Pro provide you with advanced capabilities to interact with your device, manage notifications effectively, and juggle multiple tasks with ease. By leveraging these features, you can optimize your productivity, maintain focus when need, and enhance the overall user experience on your iPhone 14 Pro.

CHAPTER 3

Phone and Messaging of iPhone 14 Pro

Making and Answering Calls:

The iPhone 14 Pro offers a comprehensive phone and messaging experience, allowing you to make and receive calls with ease. Here are some key aspects of making and answering calls on the iPhone 14 Pro:

1. Dialing a Call: To make a call, you can open the Phone app and enter the phone number using the keypad. Alternatively, you can access

your contacts and select a contact to call directly. The Phone app also provides a list of recent calls, making it easy to redial or call back a previous contact.

2. Favorites and Recent: The Phone app allows you to mark certain contacts as favorites for quick access. You can add contacts to your favorites list by selecting the star icon next to their name in the Contacts app. The Recent tab displays a chronological list of your incoming, outgoing, and missed calls.

3. VoIP Calls: The iPhone 14 Pro supports Voice over Internet Protocol (VoIP)

calls, allowing you to make calls using internet-based communication apps like FaceTime, WhatsApp, Skype, and more. These apps leverage your internet connection to make voice and video calls, providing an alternative to traditional cellular calls.

4. Call Waiting and Hold: If you're on a call and receive another incoming call, the iPhone 14 Pro supports call waiting, which notifies you of the incoming call and allows you to switch between the two calls or decline the second call. You can also place a call on hold to answer another call or perform other

tasks while keeping the
original call on hold.

5. Speakerphone and Bluetooth:
During a call, you can
activate the speakerphone by
tapping the speaker icon,
allowing you to talk and
listen without holding the
device. Additionally, you can
connect Bluetooth devices,
such as headphones or car
audio systems, to make calls
hands-free and enjoy
improved audio quality.

6. FaceTime Calls: FaceTime is
Apple's video and audio
calling service that enables
high-quality video calls
between Apple devices. With
the iPhone 14 Pro, you can

initiate FaceTime calls directly from the Phone app or the FaceTime app, allowing you to have face-to-face conversations with family, friends, or colleagues.

Voicemail:

Voicemail on the iPhone 14 Pro provides a convenient way to receive and manage voice messages when you are unable to answer a call.

1. Visual Voicemail: The iPhone 14 Pro offers Visual Voicemail, a feature that displays your voicemail messages in a visual interface within the Phone app. You can see a list of your voicemail messages,

including caller information, timestamps, and the option to play, pause, rewind, or delete messages.

2. Voicemail Transcription: With iOS 15, the iPhone 14 Pro introduces voicemail transcription, a feature that automatically transcribes your voicemail messages into text. This allows you to read the content of the voicemail without having to listen to the audio. Transcriptions can be helpful in situations where you prefer reading over listening or need to refer back to specific details mentioned in the voicemail.

3. Managing Voicemail: Within the Voicemail tab of the Phone app, you can manage your voicemail messages. This includes marking messages as read or unread, deleting messages, saving important voicemails, and sharing voicemails via messages or email.

4. Voicemail Greetings: You can customize your voicemail greeting to personalize the message callers hear when leaving a voicemail. The iPhone 14 Pro provides default voicemail greetings, or you can record a custom greeting using your own voice. This allows you to provide information or

instructions to callers, such as requesting them to leave their name and contact information.

5. Voicemail Notifications: The iPhone 14 Pro provides notifications for new voicemail messages, alerting you when a voicemail is received. You can choose to receive voicemail notifications as a badge on the Phone app, a banner notification, or a pop-up alert. Additionally, you can enable notifications to appear on the lock screen, ensuring that you never miss an important voicemail.

6. Voicemail Settings: The iPhone 14 Pro allows you to customize various voicemail settings to suit your preferences. In the Settings app, under the Phone section, you can configure options such as voicemail greeting, voicemail password, voicemail transcription, and more. These settings enable you to personalize your voicemail experience and manage voicemail-related features.

7. Carrier-Specific Voicemail: In addition to Visual Voicemail, the iPhone 14 Pro supports carrier-specific voicemail systems. Depending on your carrier,

you may have access to
additional voicemail features
and options. Carrier
voicemail systems may offer
features such as extended
voicemail storage, voice-to-
text transcriptions, voicemail
forwarding, and more.
Contact your carrier to learn
more about the specific
voicemail features available
to you.

Messaging and iMessage:

The iPhone 14 Pro offers a robust
messaging experience, allowing
you to stay connected with friends,
family, and colleagues through
various messaging platforms. Here
are some key aspects of messaging
on the iPhone 14 Pro:

1. Messages App: The Messages app is the default messaging app on the iPhone 14 Pro. It supports both traditional SMS (Short Message Service) and MMS (Multimedia Messaging Service) for communication with non-Apple devices, as well as the more advanced iMessage service for communication between Apple devices.

2. iMessage: iMessage is an enhanced messaging service exclusive to Apple devices. It allows you to send text messages, photos, videos, documents, voice messages, and more to other iOS and macOS users over an internet

connection. iMessage provides several features, including read receipts, typing indicators, message effects, and the ability to send messages over Wi-Fi or cellular data.

3. Message Effects: With iMessage, you can add special effects to your messages to enhance the visual experience. Effects include "Balloons" that fly across the screen, "Confetti" that fills the conversation, "Invisible Ink" that requires the recipient to swipe to reveal the message, and more. These effects add a touch of fun and creativity to your conversations.

4. Animoji and Memoji: The Messages app on the iPhone 14 Pro supports Animoji and Memoji, which are animated emojis and personalized emojis, respectively. Animoji uses the TrueDepth camera system to map your facial expressions onto various animal, creature, or character emojis. Memoji allows you to create custom animated emojis that resemble your appearance and express your personality.

5. Tap backs and Reactions: When receiving a message, you can use Tap backs to quickly respond with a thumbs-up, thumbs-down, heart, laughing face, or other

pre-defined reactions. This provides a convenient way to acknowledge or express your response without typing a full message.

6. Group Messaging: The Messages app allows you to create and participate in group conversations. Group messaging enables you to communicate with multiple contacts simultaneously, share messages, photos, videos, and other content, and even name the group for easier identification.

7. Message Search: With the search functionality in the Messages app, you can easily find specific messages or

conversations by entering keywords or phrases. This is especially useful when you need to locate important information or refer back to previous discussions.

FaceTime Calls:

FaceTime is Apple's video and audio calling service, designed specifically for Apple devices. It offers high-quality video and audio communication, allowing you to have face-to-face conversations with friends, family, and colleagues.

1. Video and Audio Calls: FaceTime supports both video and audio-only calls. You can initiate a FaceTime call from the FaceTime app

or directly from the Contacts app. During a video call, you can see the person you're talking to in real-time, making it feel like you're in the same room.

2. FaceTime Audio: FaceTime also provides the option for audio-only calls. This is particularly useful when you have limited bandwidth or prefer a voice-only conversation. FaceTime Audio leverages a data connection or Wi-Fi to ensure high-quality audio calls.

3. Group FaceTime: With Group FaceTime, you can have video or audio calls with multiple participants

simultaneously. Group
FaceTime allows you to
connect with up to 32 people
at once, making it ideal for
virtual meetings, family
gatherings, or socializing
with friends. Participants can
join the call using their
iPhone, iPad, Mac, or even
via the FaceTime app on the
web.

4. Spatial Audio: The iPhone 14
    Pro introduces Spatial Audio
    for FaceTime Calls. This
    feature uses advanced sound
    processing algorithms to
    create a more immersive
    audio experience during
    FaceTime calls. With Spatial
    Audio, the voices of
    participants in a group call

will sound as if they are coming from the direction of their respective video tiles, making conversations feel more natural and lifelike.

5. FaceTime Effects: Similar to iMessage, FaceTime also offers effects that you can apply during video calls to add a touch of fun and creativity. You can use filters to change your appearance, apply Animoji or Memoji to replace your face with animated emojis or personalized avatars, and use camera effects like text, stickers, and shapes to enhance your visual presence during calls.

6. Portrait Mode: The iPhone 14 Pro's advanced camera system allows you to use Portrait Mode during FaceTime calls. This feature creates a blurred background effect, focusing the attention on you and providing a professional-looking aesthetic even in video calls.

7. Screen Sharing: FaceTime now supports screen sharing, allowing you to share your iPhone's screen with the person or people you are on a call with. This is useful for collaborating, demonstrating apps or features, or simply sharing content with others during a FaceTime call.

8. FaceTime Links: With iOS 15, FaceTime introduces FaceTime Links, which enable you to schedule FaceTime calls and invite others to join using a unique link. This makes it easier to plan and initiate FaceTime calls with specific individuals or groups, even if they are not in your contacts list.

9. FaceTime on the Web: In addition to using FaceTime on your iPhone, iPad, or Mac, Apple now allows FaceTime calls to be made and received on the web. This means that you can join FaceTime calls from a browser on supported devices, expanding the

accessibility and reach of
FaceTime communication.

10.   Privacy and Security:
FaceTime is designed with
privacy and security in mind.
All FaceTime calls are end-
to-end encrypted, ensuring
that your conversations
remain private and protected.
Apple does not have access
to the content of your calls or
the ability to listen in.

CHAPTER 4

Apps and Media of iPhone 14 Pro

The iPhone 14 Pro offers a wide range of apps and media features that enhance your productivity, entertainment, and creativity. Let's explore some key aspects of the App Store, Safari web browser, Camera, and Photos app on the iPhone 14 Pro:

App Store:

The App Store is the official marketplace for apps on the iPhone 14 Pro. It provides access to a vast collection of apps, ranging from productivity tools to entertainment, games, social networking, and more. Here's what you need to know about the App Store:

1. App Discovery: The App Store features various sections and tabs that help you discover new apps. The Today tab highlights app recommendations, editor's picks, and featured content. The Apps tab provides categories, top charts, and curated collections for easy app exploration. Additionally, the Search tab allows you to search for specific apps or categories.

2. App Downloads: You can browse and download apps directly from the App Store.

When you find an app you're interested in, tap on it to access its description, screenshots, reviews, and ratings. If the app is free, you can download it instantly. For paid apps, you can purchase them securely using your Apple ID and payment method.

3. App Updates: The App Store also handles app updates, ensuring that your installed apps are up to date with the latest features and bug fixes. You can manually update apps individually or choose to enable automatic updates, which will update your apps in the background.

4. App Subscriptions: Many apps offer subscription-based services for additional features or content. The App Store manages app subscriptions, allowing you to view, manage, and cancel subscriptions easily. You can access your subscriptions in the Account section of the App Store.

5. App Privacy: Apple prioritizes user privacy and requires app developers to provide information on their app's privacy practices. The App Store displays a summary of each app's privacy practices, highlighting the data the app collects and how it is used.

This helps you make informed decisions about the apps you choose to install.

Safari Web Browser:

The Safari web browser on the iPhone 14 Pro provides a fast and secure browsing experience. It offers numerous features to enhance your web surfing and productivity.

1. Browsing Experience: Safari delivers a user-friendly and intuitive browsing experience. You can open new tabs, switch between tabs with ease, and quickly access frequently visited websites through the Favorites and Frequently Visited sections. Safari also

supports private browsing mode for enhanced privacy.

2. Tab Groups: Safari on the iPhone 14 Pro introduces Tab Groups, allowing you to organize your tabs into groups for easier navigation and multitasking. You can create custom groups, name them, and switch between different sets of tabs depending on your needs and interests.

3. Intelligent Tracking Prevention: Safari prioritizes user privacy by implementing Intelligent Tracking Prevention. This feature limits cross-site tracking, preventing advertisers and

websites from collecting your browsing history and personal information without your consent.

4. Reader View: When browsing articles or webpages with a lot of distractions, Reader View in Safari can provide a simplified reading experience. It removes ads, sidebars, and other clutter, allowing you to focus solely on the text and images of the content.

5. Extensions: Safari supports browser extensions that add additional functionality to your browsing experience. You can install extensions

from the App Store, allowing you to customize Safari with features such as ad blockers, password managers, translation tools, and more.

6. iCloud Tabs: If you use Safari on multiple Apple devices, iCloud Tabs syncs your open tabs across all your devices. This enables seamless browsing continuity, allowing you to easily switch between devices and pick up where you left off.

Camera and Photos:
The iPhone 14 Pro is equipped with advanced camera capabilities and a powerful Photos app to capture and manage your photos and videos.

Camera:

1. Camera Hardware: The iPhone 14 Pro features a high-quality camera system, including multiple lenses, sensors, and image stabilization technologies. It is designed to capture stunning photos and videos with enhanced clarity, dynamic range, and low-light performance.

2. Camera Modes: The Camera app offers various shooting modes to suit different scenarios. These include Photo mode for standard still photography, Portrait mode for creating professional-

looking portraits with depth-of-field effects, Night mode for capturing vivid photos in low-light conditions, and more. You can also access specialized modes like Panorama, Time-Lapse, and Slow Motion for unique creative possibilities.

3. ProRAW and ProRes: The iPhone 14 Pro introduces ProRAW and ProRes recording capabilities. ProRAW allows you to capture photos in a raw format, giving you more flexibility in post-processing and editing. ProRes video recording offers higher-quality video output with improved color depth and

dynamic range, ideal for professional videography.

4. Smart HDR and Deep Fusion: The Camera app utilizes advanced computational photography technologies such as Smart HDR and Deep Fusion. These features optimize exposure, detail, and noise reduction to produce vibrant and detailed photos, even in challenging lighting conditions.

5. Night Mode: With Night mode, the iPhone 14 Pro excels in capturing stunning photos in low-light environments. It automatically detects low-

light situations and extends the exposure time to gather more light, resulting in well-exposed images with reduced noise and improved clarity.

Photos:

1. Photo Organization: The Photos app on the iPhone 14 Pro organizes your photos and videos into a unified and intuitive interface. It automatically categorizes media based on dates, locations, and people, making it easy to find and revisit your favorite moments.

2. Memories: The Memories feature in the Photos app creates curated collections of your photos and videos,

intelligently selecting content based on people, places, events, and significant dates. It adds transitions, music, and other effects to turn your memories into captivating slideshows.

3. Editing Tools: The Photos app provides a comprehensive set of editing tools to enhance your photos and videos. You can adjust exposure, brightness, contrast, and color, apply filters, crop and straighten images, remove red-eye, and much more. Additionally, you can apply editing adjustments non-destructively, preserving the original image.

4. Live Photos: Live Photos brings your images to life by capturing a few seconds of video and audio before and after you press the shutter button. You can play back Live Photos with a long press, creating an engaging and immersive experience.

5. iCloud Photo Library: If you enable iCloud Photo Library, your photos and videos will be seamlessly synced across all your Apple devices. This ensures that your entire photo library is available and up to date, allowing you to access and edit your media from any device.

6. Sharing and Memories: The Photos app offers various sharing options, allowing you to easily send photos and videos to friends and family via Messages, Airdrop, or social media platforms. You can also create shared albums to collaborate and share media with specific individuals or groups.

CHAPTER 5

Personalization and Settings of iPhone14 Pro

Accessibility Features:

The iPhone 14 Pro offers a wide range of accessibility features that empower individuals with disabilities to use the device effectively. These features enhance usability, visibility, and interaction options. Here are some key accessibility features:

1. voiceover: voiceover is a screen reader that provides spoken feedback to users

with visual impairments. It audibly describes on-screen elements, allowing users to navigate the interface, interact with apps, and read text.

2. Magnifier: The Magnifier feature turns the iPhone 14 Pro into a digital magnifying glass. It utilizes the device's camera to zoom in on objects, providing enhanced visibility for users with low vision.

3. Display Accommodations: The iPhone 14 Pro includes display accommodations such as Invert Colors, Color Filters, and Smart Invert, which help users with visual sensitivities or color

blindness by adjusting the display to their preferences.

4. Assistive Touch: Assistive Touch offers customizable gestures and virtual buttons that enable users with motor disabilities to navigate and interact with the device using alternative input methods.

5. Switch Control: Switch Control allows users with physical disabilities to control their iPhone 14 Pro using external adaptive switches or the device's built-in sensors. It offers customizable scanning options and gesture controls.

Privacy and Security Settings:

The iPhone 14 Pro prioritizes user privacy and provides a range of privacy and security settings to protect your data. Here are some key privacy and security features:

1. App Permissions: You have control over the permissions granted to apps on your iPhone 14 Pro. You can manage app access to features such as camera, microphone, location, contacts, and more, ensuring that apps only access what is necessary.

2. Privacy Labels: The App Store displays privacy labels for apps, providing

information on the data they collect and how it is used. This transparency helps you make informed decisions about the apps you install.

3. Intelligent Tracking Prevention: Safari's Intelligent Tracking Prevention restricts cross-site tracking, preventing advertisers from collecting your browsing history and personal information without your consent.

4. Face ID and Touch ID: The iPhone 14 Pro supports Face ID facial recognition or Touch ID fingerprint recognition, providing secure authentication methods for

unlocking your device,
making purchases, and
accessing sensitive data.

5. Secure Enclave and Data
Encryption: The iPhone 14
Pro's Secure Enclave protects
your biometric data and
secures sensitive information.
Additionally, all data stored
on the device is encrypted,
ensuring that even if your
device is lost or stolen, your
data remains secure.

Battery and Power Management:

To optimize battery life and
manage power usage on the iPhone
14 Pro, you can take advantage of
various features and settings:

1. Battery Health: The Battery Health feature provides insights into the health of your iPhone's battery. It displays the maximum capacity of the battery and indicates if it is operating at peak performance or if it may need to be replaced.

2. Low Power Mode: When your battery is running low, enabling Low Power Mode helps conserve power by reducing background activity, optimizing system performance, and reducing visual effects.

3. Background App Refresh: You can manage the background refresh behavior

of apps to minimize their
impact on battery life.
Selectively enable or disable
background refresh for
specific apps or choose to
completely disable it for all
apps.

4. Optimized Battery Charging:
   This feature helps extend the
   overall battery lifespan by
   reducing the time your
   iPhone 14 Pro spends fully
   charged. It learns your
   charging patterns and
   intelligently charges the
   battery to minimize the time
   it stays at 100%.

Software Updates:

The iPhone 14 Pro benefits from
regular software updates that

introduce new features,
improvements, and security
patches.

1. iOS Updates: iOS updates
   bring new features,
   enhancements, and bug fixes
   to the iPhone 14 Pro. They
   are designed to improve the
   performance, security, and
   overall user experience of the
   device. When a new iOS
   update becomes available,
   you will receive a
   notification, and you can
   choose to install it over-the-
   air directly on your iPhone 14
   Pro.

2. Automatic Updates: You
   have the option to enable
   automatic updates on your

iPhone 14 Pro. When this feature is turned on, your device will automatically download and install iOS updates in the background, ensuring that you always have the latest software version without manual intervention.

3. App Updates: In addition to iOS updates, the App Store also provides updates for individual apps installed on your iPhone 14 Pro. These app updates deliver bug fixes, performance improvements, new features, and compatibility enhancements. You can choose to update your apps manually or enable

automatic updates for apps as well.

4. Backup Before Updating: It is recommended to back up your iPhone 14 Pro before installing any software updates. Backing up your device ensures that your data, settings, and preferences are securely saved, allowing you to restore them if needed.

5. Security Patches: Software updates often include important security patches to address vulnerabilities and protect your iPhone 14 Pro from potential threats. It is crucial to install updates promptly to ensure that your device remains secure and

protected against emerging security risks.

6. Update Settings: You can customize your update settings on the iPhone 14 Pro. This includes options to automatically download updates, schedule update installations, enable automatic app updates, and more. By accessing the Software Update section in the Settings app, you can manage how and when updates are installed on your device.

Regular software updates on the iPhone 14 Pro keep your device up to date with the latest features, enhancements, and security measures. By staying current with updates, you can enjoy the best performance, improved functionality, and a secure mobile experience.

CHAPTER 6

Advanced Features of iPhone 14 Pro

iCloud and Apple ID:

1. iCloud Storage: iPhone 14 Pro integrates seamlessly with iCloud, Apple's cloud storage service. iCloud allows you to securely store and sync your photos, videos, documents, contacts, calendars, and more across all your Apple devices. You can also access your files from a web browser on any computer.

2. iCloud Backup: With iCloud Backup, you can automatically back up your iPhone 14 Pro's data to iCloud. This includes your device settings, app data, photos, videos, and more. In the event of a lost or damaged device, you can restore your data to a new iPhone easily.

3. iCloud Drive: iCloud Drive enables file storage and synchronization across devices. You can access your files from the Files app on your iPhone 14 Pro, making it easy to work on documents, presentations, spreadsheets, and other files from anywhere.

4. Find My: The Find My app helps you locate your iPhone 14 Pro if it is lost or stolen. It also allows you to track the location of your friends and family who share their location with you. You can remotely lock, erase, or play a sound on your device for added security.

Apple Pay:

1. Digital Wallet: iPhone 14 Pro supports Apple Pay, a convenient and secure way to make payments using your device. With Apple Pay, you can add your credit or debit cards to the Wallet app and make contactless payments at supported retailers, online stores, and in apps.

2. Face ID or Touch ID
   Authentication: Apple Pay
   uses the biometric
   authentication features of the
   iPhone 14 Pro, such as Face
   ID or Touch ID, to authorize
   payments securely. You can
   simply authenticate yourself
   using your face or fingerprint
   to complete a transaction.

3. Apple Pay Cash: Apple Pay
   Cash allows you to send and
   receive money with friends
   and family directly from the
   Messages app. You can use
   the funds to make purchases,
   transfer them to your bank
   account, or keep them as a
   balance for future
   transactions.

Airdrop and File Sharing:

1. Airdrop: Airdrop enables fast and easy file sharing between Apple devices, including the iPhone 14 Pro. You can wirelessly transfer photos, videos, documents, links, and other files to nearby devices using Wi-Fi and Bluetooth. Airdrop ensures encrypted and secure file transfers.

2. Share Sheet: The Share Sheet feature allows you to quickly share content from apps on your iPhone 14 Pro. With a few taps, you can share photos, videos, links, documents, and more via AirDrop, Messages, email, social media platforms, or other compatible apps.

Augmented Reality (AR) Apps:

1. ARKit: The iPhone 14 Pro leverages ARKit, Apple's augmented reality platform, to deliver immersive and interactive AR experiences. ARKit enables developers to create AR apps that overlay virtual objects and information onto the real world, enhancing gaming, education, shopping, and other applications.

2. AR Apps: The App Store offers a wide range of AR apps that take advantage of the iPhone 14 Pro's capabilities. These apps allow you to explore virtual worlds,

view 3D models, measure distances, try on virtual furniture, play AR games, and much more.

3. AR Quick Look: With AR Quick Look, you can preview and interact with 3D models in the real world. By simply tapping on a compatible file or link, you can view and manipulate virtual objects, helping you make informed decisions about purchases or visualizing designs.

The advanced features of iPhone 14 Pro, including iCloud and Apple ID integration, Apple Pay, Airdrop and file sharing, and augmented reality capabilities, enhance your productivity, security, and creativity. These features provide seamless connectivity, convenient payment options, efficient file sharing, and immersive augmented reality experiences, making the iPhone 14 Pro a versatile and powerful device.

CHAPTER 7

Troubleshooting of iPhone Pro 14

While the iPhone 14 Pro is a reliable device, you may encounter occasional issues. Here are some common troubleshooting steps to resolve common problems:

1. Restart your iPhone: A simple restart can often resolve minor software glitches. Press and hold the power button until the "Slide to power off" option appears. Slide the power off slider, wait a few seconds, then press and hold the power

button again to turn it back on.

2. Update iOS: Keeping your iPhone's software up to date is important for stability and bug fixes. Go to Settings > General > Software Update to check if any updates are available. If an update is available, download and install it.

3. Force Restart: If your iPhone becomes unresponsive or frozen, a force restart may help. The method to force restart varies depending on the iPhone model. For the iPhone 14 Pro, quickly press and release the volume up button, then quickly press

and release the volume down button. Finally, press and hold the side button until the Apple logo appears.

4. Clear Storage: If you're experiencing performance issues or running out of storage, consider deleting unnecessary apps, photos, videos, or other files. Go to Settings > General > iPhone Storage to view and manage your storage usage. You can offload unused apps or use cloud storage services like iCloud or Google Drive to store your files.

5. Reset Settings: If you're facing persistent issues, resetting your iPhone's

settings can help. Go to
Settings > General > Reset >
Reset All Settings. Note that
this will reset all your
settings to their factory
defaults, but your data and
media will remain intact.

6. Restore from Backup: If all
   else fails, you can restore
   your iPhone from a backup.
   Ensure you have a recent
   backup available through
   iCloud or iTunes. Go to
   Settings > General > Reset >
   Erase All Content and
   Settings. After the reset,
   follow the on-screen prompts
   to restore your iPhone from
   the backup.

7. Contact Apple Support: If you've tried the above steps and the issue persists, it may be necessary to contact Apple Support for further assistance. They can provide personalized guidance and help troubleshoot more complex issues.

   Troubleshooting steps may vary depending on the specific problem you're facing. It's always a good idea to consult Apple's official support documentation or reach out to their support channels for accurate and detailed troubleshooting guidance.

8. Network Troubleshooting: If you're experiencing network-related issues, such as Wi-Fi or cellular connectivity problems, try the following:

- Restart your router or modem to refresh the network connection.

- Toggle Airplane Mode on and off to reset your device's wireless connections.

- Forget and reconnect to the Wi-Fi network you're having trouble with.

- Ensure that you have a stable internet connection by testing

on different networks
or contacting your
service provider.

- Reset network settings
  on your iPhone by
  going to Settings >
  General > Reset >
  Reset Network
  Settings. Note that this
  will remove saved Wi-
  Fi passwords and other
  network-related
  settings.

9. Battery Performance: If
   you're facing battery drain
   issues, consider the following
   steps to optimize battery
   performance:

- Check battery usage in
  Settings > Battery to

identify apps or services consuming excessive power. You can close unnecessary background apps or adjust their settings to minimize battery usage.

- Disable unnecessary features like background app refresh, push email, location services, and automatic downloads.

- Reduce screen brightness or enable auto-brightness.

- Enable Low Power Mode in Settings > Battery to conserve

battery life when the charge is low.

- Disable unnecessary notifications or customize their settings in Settings > Notifications.

10.   App Issues: If a specific app is causing problems, try these troubleshooting steps:

- Update the app to the latest version from the App Store.

- Force closes the problematic app and reopen it.

- Delete and reinstall the app if the issue persists.

- Check if the app has any known compatibility issues with your iPhone model or iOS version.

- Contact the app developer for further assistance or check their support resources.

11. Hardware Issues: If you suspect a hardware problem with your iPhone 14 Pro, such as unresponsive buttons or malfunctioning camera, consider the following:

- Ensure your iPhone is free from any physical damage or water exposure.

- Check if the issue persists in different apps or under different circumstances.

- Visit an authorized Apple service provider or contact Apple Support for hardware diagnosis and repair options.